LONDON'S RAILWAY STATIONS

Oliver Green

SHIRE PUBLICATIONS

Bloomsbury Publishing Plc

Kemp House, Chawley Park, Cumnor Hill, Oxford OX2 9PH, UK

29 Earlsfort Terrace, Dublin 2, Ireland

1385 Broadway, 5th Floor, New York, NY 10018, USA

E-mail: shire@bloomsbury.com

www.shirebooks.co.uk

SHIRE is a trademark of Osprey Publishing Ltd

First published in Great Britain in 2022

A catalogue record for this book is available from the British Library.

ISBN: PB 978 1 78442 505 0
        eBook 978 1 78442 506 7
        ePDF 978 1 78442 504 3
        XML 978 1 78442 503 6

22 23 24 25 26   10 9 8 7 6 5 4 3 2 1

Typeset by PDQ Digital Media Solutions, Bungay, UK

Printed and bound in India by Replika Press Private Ltd.

Shire Publications supports the Woodland Trust, the UK's leading woodland conservation charity.

COVER IMAGE

Front cover: St. Pancras International Station in 2014, when it hosted David Batchelor's colourful artwork 'Chromolocomotion'. A permanent statue of John Betjeman can be seen in the foreground and beyond, Paul Day's 'The Meeting Place' shows a giant couple embracing under the station clock. (Alamy) Back cover: Art deco LNER luggage label for use on the streamlined Silver Jubilee service from Newcastle to King's Cross, 1935. (Oliver Green)

TITLE PAGE IMAGE

Charing Cross from above in 2009, showing the huge size of the 1980s Embankment Place office development by Terry Farrell, which wraps under and over the station. In the foreground are the footbridges opened on both sides of Hungerford Railway Bridge in 2003.

ACKNOWLEDGEMENTS

Copyright in the images is acknowledged as follows:

Alamy, page 49 (bottom); citytransportinfo-Public Domain, page 1; Culture Club/Getty Images, page 14; Dan Kitwood/Getty Images, page 52; English Heritage/Heritage Images/Getty Images, pages 26, 39 (bottom); Fraselpantz/Public Domain, page 28; Grimshaw Architects, pages 6, 45; GrindtXX/CC BY-SA 4.0, page 47; Hufton+Crow/View Pictures/Universal Images Group via Getty Images, page 32 (top); Hulton Archive/Getty Images, pages 58 (bottom), 59; Museum of London/Heritage Images/Getty Images, page 42 (bottom); Oliver Green, pages 11, 12 (both), 13, 16, 17, 22, 32 (bottom), 33, 38, 39 (top), 40, 43, 44, 50, 53 (bottom); Philafrenzy/CC-BY-SA-4.0, page 23; Rail Photo/Construction Photography/Avalon/Getty Images, page 49 (top); SSPL/Getty Images, pages 5, 7, 9, 18, 19, 20, 25, 29, 30, 31, 34, 35, 36, 42 (top), 46, 48, 51, 53 (top), 55, 56, 57, 58 (top), 60; © TfL from the London Transport Museum collection, page 10; Train Photos/CC BY-SA 2.0, page 61.

CONTENTS

INTRODUCTION

LONDON HAS MORE main line railway stations than any other city in the world. Its earliest terminals opened in the late 1830s when lines between the capital and the regions were built during the first railway boom. The original station at London Bridge, the capital's first passenger terminus, opened in December 1836, six months before the young Victoria came to the throne. The last main line, terminating at Marylebone, opened in March 1899, two years before the elderly queen died.

Over six decades, 15 railway terminals were built in London, an astonishing number that is not equalled by any other city in the world. By 1901, London's railway infrastructure, built up throughout the Victorian period, was enormous. Stations, depots, yards, tracks, tunnels, bridges and other railway facilities such as hotels, warehouses and stables, covered huge areas of the capital. London had become a railway city, totally dependent on railways to function as a commercial, financial and industrial metropolis.

The great railway termini were the most obvious and visible features of the railway network. In the free-enterprise culture of the nineteenth century, the Government was not directly involved in planning, financing or managing railway development, but Parliament had a crucial role in authorising every project. Each proposed new line and terminus required a private Act of Parliament to give the railway company power to buy land by compulsory

The 'black cathedral' in steam days by Edward Bawden, showing the network of high-level walkways at Liverpool Street.

purchase. To secure this, every plan had to face detailed scrutiny from Parliamentary committees and, occasionally, Royal Commissions.

Railway development in London was particularly contentious and was complicated by issues of property ownership and the physical geography of the city. Throughout the nineteenth century, plans for London termini came to involve more than a dozen separate railway companies, often battling for access to adjacent station sites, but with little collaboration between them. They were also up against powerful obstruction from wealthy landowners and authorities such as the City of London Corporation, which wanted to limit the railways' encroachment on the central areas of the City and Westminster. The result was a ring of main-line termini all round the central districts of London. Inside that ring, roughly marked out by what is now London Underground's Circle Line, rail access was only really opened up by the electric Tube lines built in the early 1900s. Of the 15 termini only two, Broad Street and Holborn Viaduct, have been closed and demolished.

More than a century later, two additional main lines are under development to bring high-speed trains to and from the capital. Although both are completely new railways on physically separate alignments from the Victorian main lines,

An architect's view of how Euston 3 may emerge by 2030.

both will operate from existing termini that have been rebuilt and extended. High Speed One (HS1) was opened to the renamed St. Pancras International in 2007 and a new station alongside Euston is now under construction for HS2, due to open in the late 2020s.

This book is a short history of London's 13 existing terminals, laid out as a journey around central London, starting at Paddington in the north west and travelling clockwise. Most of the stations described are served by, or are close to, London Underground's Circle Line, which was originally intended to link the main-line terminals. This is the easiest way to travel on the circuit (with a Travelcard), although cycling is cheaper and probably quicker. Line changes or short walks are needed to get to Marylebone, Fenchurch Street or London Bridge.

THE STATIONS

PADDINGTON

Paddington is the best preserved of London's Victorian terminals. To step off a train under Isambard Kingdom Brunel's great triple-span iron-and-glass roof is one of the most dramatic ways to arrive in London.

What we see now is not the original terminus of the Great Western Railway (GWR). The line was built in the 1830s to link London with Bristol. In 1835, when work began on the section of line just west of London, the final site of the terminus had not been chosen. Brunel, as the GWR's chief engineer, had discussions with Robert Stephenson, whose London & Birmingham Railway (L&BR) was approaching from the north west, about creating a joint terminus at Euston. However, no agreement could be reached and the L&BR occupied the Euston site alone.

Brunel already favoured Paddington, probably because the site was adjacent to the basin of the Grand Junction Canal, which had opened there in 1801, followed by the Regents

The first station at Paddington opened in 1838 and was replaced by a goods depot when the present terminus opened in 1854. This is now the site of the Paddington Central office complex between the railway and the canal.

Canal in 1820. The potential for trans-shipment of goods on to canals was an important consideration for early railways and the two canals here had already encouraged the rapid growth of Paddington from a village into the developed western edge of London.

The GWR could only afford to build a rather small wooden passenger terminus for the opening of the line in 1838. It stood just north of the current station on the site now occupied by the high-rise office development, Paddington Central, between the railway and the canal. The low-level cutting alongside Eastbourne Terrace, where the present station stands, was originally used as a goods shed. Later, the areas used for the permanent passenger station and a larger goods depot were effectively swapped over.

The first Paddington has been described as a makeshift affair. Architecturally, it was no match for Euston, and passenger facilities were very basic. Services to Maidenhead started in June 1838, extending to Reading in 1840 and through to Bristol in 1841. On 13 June 1842, Queen Victoria herself travelled by train for the first time, between Slough and Paddington, announcing that she was 'quite charmed' with the experience.

As the GWR's traffic grew, the temporary terminus soon proved inadequate. In 1850, Brunel was asked to design a much larger new station on the present Paddington site. Building technology had moved on and Brunel's second station was clearly influenced by Joseph Paxton's revolutionary iron-and-glass Crystal Palace, designed for the Great Exhibition of 1851 – an early example of pre-fabrication.

In January 1851, Brunel wrote excitedly to the architect Matthew Digby Wyatt, who was secretary of the exhibition committee: 'I am going to design, in a great hurry ... a Station after my own fancy ... it is at Paddington, in a cutting, and admitting of no exterior, all interior and all roofed in.' Brunel asked Wyatt to act as his assistant on the decorative details and together they approached the engineering contractors Fox Henderson, who had worked on the exhibition building in Hyde Park, to construct the new trainshed.

In December 1851, the GWR engaged another architect, Philip Hardwick, who had just completed the Great Hall at Euston, to design a large hotel in front of the station on Praed Street. The grand new Paddington station and Great Western Royal Hotel were both completed and opened in 1854.

Brunel rarely relaxed, which makes John Doubleday's 1982 statue of the great engineer, now positioned between the central platforms at Paddington, seem a little inappropriate. Brunel sits surveying the impressive interior of his trainshed, an unlikely pose for such a workaholic, but he is clutching his famous stovepipe hat in his left hand, ready to rush off to another site inspection.

Brunel's second Paddington is a light and elegant design, but also an extremely sound and functional piece of engineering. The roof of the station consists of three parallel transepts, each 700ft long, making it the largest trainshed in existence at the time. A fourth longitudinal span was added in 1913–16, mimicking Brunel's style, but built of steel rather than iron. Wyatt's main contribution as architectural collaborator was the attractive metal tracery on the end-screens of the trainshed, the decorative embellishments of the columns and arches, and the two sets of oriel windows on the first floor of the office buildings overlooking Platform 1.

Hardwick's Great Western Royal Hotel at Paddington opened at the same time as the station in 1854. Brunel's trainsheds are on the left.

UNDERGROUND
PADDINGTON
NEW STATION
BOOK TO
ALL PARTS OF LONDON
MOVING STAIRCASE
SUBWAY CONNECTION.
OPENS
DECEMBER 1ST
LINKS THE G.W.R.
WITH ALL PARTS OF
LONDON.
1012 1000 10 11 13
WATERLOW & SONS LTD LITH LONDON WALL LONDON
ELECTRIC RAILWAY HOUSE, BROADWAY, WESTMINSTER, S.W.

In the 1930s, GWR architect Percy Culverhouse gutted the Victorian hotel, replacing its large over-decorated rooms and coffee house with a modish art-deco style interior. He also added extensions to the hotel and a *moderne* office block beside the Praed Street ramp. This still proclaims 'GWR PADDINGTON' in giant raised letters at the top of the building.

The whole of the station interior has been refurbished, repaired and dramatically re-lit in the twenty-first century, revealing Brunel and Wyatt's beautiful roof structure and decorative detailing, hidden for years under the grime left by steam trains. The infrastructure around the station has also been renovated and refurbished, including the former Metropolitan platforms at Bishops Road, which now have a spacious booking hall above them and a new exit to the Paddington Central complex. This area has come full circle, having once housed the original 1838 station, and later the temporary terminus of the world's first underground railway, opened in 1863, and now part of London Underground's Hammersmith & City Line.

OPPOSITE
Poster advertising the new Bakerloo Tube station at Paddington, one of the first with 'moving staircases' (escalators), 1913.

Art deco Paddington. This GWR office block built in the 1930s still has its original lettering and lighting.

The first electric trains at Paddington on the Heathrow Express service, introduced in 1998. The original fleet was replaced in 2020.

Paddington's attractive blend of restored heritage and striking modernity continues in its latest development, the Crossrail project, opening in 2022 as the Elizabeth Line. This new railway under central London leaves the GWR main line just outside Paddington and dives below the West End

Heritage and modernity at Paddington, 2021: one of GWR's new bi-mode Hitachi express trains under Brunel's cleaned, painted and relit 1854 trainshed.

and City in main-line size Tube tunnels, surfacing again in east and south-east London. The platforms at Paddington are on the Eastbourne Terrace axis of the station, alongside Brunel's trainshed.

MARYLEBONE

Marylebone was built as the terminus of the last main line into London in the nineteenth century, which brought the Great Central Railway (GCR) into the capital. The station was opened on 15 March 1899. It was never a great success and in the early 1980s a plan to convert the rail line into a coach route, with Marylebone as a bus station, was given serious consideration. Fortunately this idea was dropped and a major programme of investment began in the 1990s. Marylebone's future prospects now look better than at any time in the twentieth century.

The driving force behind the original project was Sir Edward Watkin, one of the most far sighted of the Victorian railway barons. Watkin was chairman of the Manchester, Sheffield & Lincolnshire Railway (MS&LR) and had grandiose plans to extend its main line through the Midlands to London.

Postcard of a Sheffield & Manchester express at Marylebone, c.1905.

The MS&LR's change of name in 1897 to the Great Central Railway confirmed the scale of his ambition. Watkin was already chairman of both the Metropolitan and South Eastern Railways, and of a company planning to build a tunnel under the English Channel. His ultimate aim was to link all these projects together to create a rail route from Manchester to Paris.

Preparations for the final approach to Marylebone were both costly and controversial. The GCR built six large tenement blocks just off St. John's Wood Road to rehouse about 3,000 of nearly 4,500 people whose homes had to be demolished. The railway goods yard included a massive five-storey warehouse, which was later destroyed in a bombing raid in 1941. Both the GCR housing and the entire Marylebone goods yard were cleared in the 1970s to create the Lisson Green social housing estate.

Postcard view of Marylebone station concourse, 1907.

There was a much bigger fuss about the need to build the railway under Lord's, home of the Marylebone Cricket Club (MCC). When word got out in 1890 of the threat to the

GREAT CENTRAL STATION (MARYLEBONE, LONDON)

sacred turf, *Punch* magazine published a cartoon showing the eminent batsman W.G. Grace leading his cricket team out to meet their enemy: Watkin and the railway navvies.

To placate the MCC, Watkin guaranteed that all necessary work would be carried out between the end of one cricketing season and the start of the next. Work started on 1 September 1896. The turf was removed, the tunnels excavated at record speed, and the reinstated pitch was handed back eight months later, on 8 May 1897. Not one day's play was lost.

Because of the high expense of getting its line to Marylebone, the GCR economised on its passenger terminus. The station buildings were designed not by an architect but by one of the company's engineering staff, H.W. Braddock. It is a modest construction in red brick, hidden from the Marylebone Road by the enormous bulk of the Great Central Hotel. As railway historian Alan Jackson aptly commented, 'the result would have been creditable as council offices for a minor provincial town, but was hardly worthy as the London terminus of a railway that aspired to be in the first rank'.

An elegant iron-and-glass canopy over the entrance yard connects the station with the Great Central Hotel. As the railway had run out of money, the hotel was financed as a separate enterprise by Sir John Blundell Maple. The architect was Colonel Robert William Edis, who spared no expense on the lavish design. The nine-storey hotel was built around a great glazed central courtyard and there was even a cycle track on the roof for energetic guests.

The Great Central Hotel opened four months after the station, on 1 July 1899. It is unlikely that the 700 bedrooms were ever fully booked, and traffic through the station could not have filled them. At this time there were just 11 trains a day scheduled each way in and out of Marylebone, seven of them expresses to and from Manchester. The trains were luxurious but slow, and the GCR's station porters were often said to outnumber the passengers.

The clock tower of the former Great Central Hotel, Marylebone, now the Landmark London.

The GCR never became a serious challenger to the other well-established main-line companies with long-distance services to the North. However, it did develop successful outer suburban services which became Marylebone's mainstay. These were run in agreement with the Metropolitan Railway over the joint line to Aylesbury and with the GWR over its newly opened route through High Wycombe from 1906. Both lines became popular with more affluent Edwardian commuters, who were encouraged to move out to growing country towns such as Beaconsfield and Gerrards Cross.

The GCR disappeared altogether in 1923, when it became part of the London & North Eastern Railway (LNER). In the following year, traffic through Marylebone was boosted by the British Empire Exhibition at Wembley, for which a ten-minute service of non-stop trains was introduced. Sporting events at the new Wembley Stadium, first used for the FA Cup Final in 1923, also brought large crowds through Marylebone, but these busy occasions only punctuated long periods of quiet.

After nationalisation in 1948, the Great Central Hotel became the headquarters of the British Transport Commission and later of British Railways (BR). The grand public rooms were stripped of their decorative features and the increasingly dowdy interior came to look like any other faceless government offices. Railway staff referred to it as 'the Kremlin'. BR eventually moved out in 1991 and the building was sold for restoration as a luxury hotel. The extensively renovated building re-opened as the Landmark London in 1995.

Marylebone continued to slumber through the 1960s and 1970s, but when BR moved to close the station in the 1980s this was strongly opposed. Marylebone was reprieved and Network South East, BR's new regional sector, announced an £85 million 'total route modernisation project' for the station and line. By the 1990s, Marylebone was being completely refurbished with a new terrazzo-style passenger concourse, a reduced footprint for the platforms and all services upgraded.

When BR was privatised in 1996, Chiltern Railways, the new operator, was in a strong position to develop the business. Passenger numbers have grown rapidly, long-distance services to the West Midlands have been introduced and a new link via Bicester has enabled Chiltern to introduce direct services to Oxford. The remarkable renaissance of Marylebone looks set to continue.

Marylebone station frontage in 2010. The canopy in the centre runs across to the former Great Central Hotel, now reopened as the Landmark London.

EUSTON

The original station opened at Euston in July 1837 was London's first inter-city main-line passenger terminus. The L&BR, engineered by Robert Stephenson, brought the Midlands, and later the whole of the north west, within easy reach of London for the first time. Euston is still London's main rail gateway to and from the north west, but no trace of the original station survived the comprehensive redevelopment of the 1960s.

The railway authorised by Parliament in 1833 was to terminate at Camden, but a year later the L&BR got permission for an extension that took the line across the Regent's Canal and just over a mile closer to central London. This meant that the first section from Euston up to Camden had to be built on a severe gradient. Early steam locomotives would have had difficulty climbing Camden Bank, so Stephenson decided to use cable haulage instead. Trains leaving Euston were pulled up to Camden by cable, where steam locomotives took over for the journey north. The cable system was abandoned in

London's first inter-city terminus at Euston, 1837. This is the original trainshed designed by engineer Charles Fox. Initially all trains were cable-hauled up to Camden, where a steam locomotive took over.

1844, but for many years afterwards trains had to be double headed out of Euston or pushed by a second engine at the rear. The site at Camden became a large goods depot with transfer facilities on to the canal, extensive horse stabling and an engine shed, now the Roundhouse arts centre.

The passenger terminus at Euston was quite basic when it opened in 1837. The operational part consisted of two wooden platforms known as the arrival and departure stages. There were four tracks covered by a simple 200ft cast-iron-and-glass trainshed, the first of its kind, designed by structural engineer Charles Fox. The station offices were alongside the departure platform, behind which an avenue was laid out from the Euston Road to the station. Here a great Doric portico and screen, designed by architect Philip Hardwick, was completed in 1838. This portico served no practical purpose, but it was an impressive 'gateway to the north' and a powerful symbol of the coming railway age.

In 1846 the L&BR became part of a larger company, the London & North Western Railway (LNWR). Hardwick's son, also called Philip, was commissioned to extend and improve the company's London terminus, but once again architectural grandeur seemed to trump practicality. Hardwick junior designed a monumental Great Hall, placed in the centre of the Euston site beyond his father's gateway. As journalist Samuel Sidney wrote in 1851, just two years after it opened,

'Comfort has been sacrificed to magnificence ... a vast hall with magnificent roof and scagliola pillars appears to have swallowed up all the money and all the light of the establishment'.

The Great Hall and portico effectively split the station site, making it difficult to expand the number of platforms, while the original vision of a grand avenue up to the 'arch' was soon blocked by the infill of a dull hotel extension. The interior of the Great Hall took up too much space as an over-grand waiting room but had no useful facilities for passengers.

A scheme for the complete reconstruction of Euston was first considered in the 1890s, but the only improvements were piecemeal, such as the introduction of Tube connections in 1907 and electrification of the suburban service to Watford in 1922. A year later the LNWR became part of the London, Midland & Scottish Railway (LMS), largest of the 'Big Four'. A substantial art-deco styled headquarters for the company's staff was built alongside Euston on Eversholt Street, but plans for a new station got no further than an impressive architect's perspective.

When BR took over in 1948 there was money to redecorate the Great Hall, but nothing more. Then in 1959 comprehensive rebuilding of Euston was on the agenda again as part of BR's full scale modernisation and electrification of the main lines to Birmingham, Manchester and Liverpool. The plans included the destruction of both Euston's grand monuments, the Great Hall and the Doric Arch. The loss of the Great Hall was probably inevitable as it stood in the way of a rational platform layout and could not have been moved. Dismantling the Euston Arch for re-erection elsewhere would have been possible but there was no official inclination to do so.

This became the first big conservation battle of the sixties, at a time when modernism was in vogue and there was little interest in adapting or preserving Victorian buildings. The fight was taken all the way to the prime

OPPOSITE
The magnificent Great Hall at Euston, designed by Philip Hardwick junior in 1846. It is seen here as refurbished in the 1950s, only to be demolished by BR in 1962.

Euston 2, opened by the Queen in 1968, is overseen here by Robert Stephenson's statue (right). Centre left, beyond the station, is the former LMS head office, Euston House, built in the 1930s.

minister, Harold Macmillan, by the Royal Academy, the Victorian Society and many architectural writers, such as John Betjeman. But Macmillan would not intervene and the complete demolition of everything at old Euston was carried out with almost indecent haste in 1961–2.

The new Euston, designed by BR architect Ray Moorcroft, was opened in 1968. It was far more functional than the previous motley collection of buildings on the site, but as architecture it is dull and uninspiring. The central hall appears to be based on the 'passenger flow' planning of 1960s airports, but with none of the facilities that airline passengers expect, such as comfortable seating and easy access.

Work is now under way to create Euston 3, starting with a new terminus for HS2, the controversial high-speed line between London, the Midlands and the North. When the first section opens in the late 2020s, trains will run from Birmingham to a new station at Old Oak Common in west London. This will provide interchange with the Elizabeth Line and London Overground. The new HS2 station at Euston, to be reached by new tunnels under north London, is being built to the west of the existing station, which will be modified and rebuilt to minimise disruption to current services. Two of the unloved office towers built in front of Euston in the 1970s have already been demolished and the idea of resurrecting the Euston Arch may even be considered.

Euston 2's concourse and departure board in 2018. There is a spacious green marble floor but no passenger seating. This will be remodelled or demolished as the new station is developed.

ST. PANCRAS

St. Pancras was already seen as a symbol of the age when it was first built. A writer in *Building News* claimed in 1875 that 'Railway termini and hotels are to the nineteenth century what monasteries and cathedrals were to the thirteenth century. They are truly the only representative buildings we possess.'

St. Pancras was to the Victorians, and remains to this day, the most spectacular of the great London railway stations. The trainshed and the hotel at St. Pancras were designed separately by an engineer and an architect, both working on the largest possible scale at the time. These buildings were a grandiose statement of a railway company's ambition, but they were also a very practical and harmonious combination of elements. Over time the hotel in particular became widely viewed as a high Victorian folly that no longer served a useful purpose, yet it could not be severed from the station. After decades of blight and uncertainty, both halves of this magnificent edifice have at last been restored and adapted to new use in the twenty-first century. St. Pancras will not suffer the same ignominious fate as Euston.

St. Pancras station was a late arrival in London, created not out of need but because the Midland Railway (MR) wanted to have its own passenger terminal in the capital. In 1858 the company started running goods and coal trains from the industrial East Midlands to London over the Great Northern Railway (GNR) main line. As traffic grew, the company soon decided to build its own goods depot just north of King's Cross, and by 1863 had plans to reach this with its own new London Extension line. The project grew from being primarily about freight access into a full-scale passenger main line, which of course required a suitably grand London terminus as well as a goods depot.

The MR's London Extension line, built in the 1860s, was designed by the MR's consulting engineer, William Henry Barlow, who also planned the layout and infrastructure of the large terminus and goods station complex just north of the Euston Road. This was as close to central London as Parliament would permit the MR to build. It still required massive property demolition on the route through Camden, and in the areas known as Agar Town and Somers Town, which had grown up since the arrival of the first trunk line to nearby Euston thirty years earlier.

Seven streets of housing were demolished with no offer of compensation or rehousing for the thousands evicted from their homes. There was a greater outcry at the way navvies began to cut through old St. Pancras churchyard to make way for the railway, carelessly scattering rotten coffins and human remains. The young Thomas Hardy, then training as an architect, was given the task of supervising this exhumation work over several nights. He later recalled the experience in a poem of 1882 called 'The Levelled Churchyard'. The gravestones that were removed can still be seen stacked round a single tree in the churchyard, now known as the Hardy Tree.

Having bridged the canal, Barlow's main line approached the Euston Road at high level rather than coming down to

street level on a steep gradient like the route into Euston. The
approach also contrasts with the GNR, which had run into
King's Cross in tunnels *under* the Regent's Canal.

Barlow deliberately planned for his station platforms to
be at first floor level above a large ground floor undercroft.
An enormous single-span cast-iron roof – the tallest and
widest ever built – was constructed using a massive wooden
frame that was moved across the station deck on rails as work
progressed. In the basement, cast-iron pillars supporting the
deck were divided into a grid based on the dimensions of the
brewery warehouses in Burton-upon-Trent. The MR planned
to run three special beer trains a day from the Midlands to
St. Pancras. Individual goods wagons would be lowered into
the vaults by hydraulic lift and unloaded onto horse-drawn
drays for delivery to pubs all over London.

All this could be done without passengers and goods
crossing one another's paths as happened at most busy rail
terminals. Barlow's station plan was a brilliant use of space
and logistics. Most other goods traffic, including milk and

Cutaway view of
St. Pancras under
construction
from the
Illustrated Times,
1868, showing
the great
trainshed being
built over the
platform floor
deck and the
basement area
designed for
beer barrels, now
used by Eurostar
passengers.

coal, came into the large goods yard built just to the west of the passenger station. This is the space occupied in the twenty-first century by the British Library and the Francis Crick Institute for biomedical research, which are both on former railway land. The ground floor of the station is now the Eurostar terminal.

The Midland chose the architect for their Grand Hotel by holding a competition in 1865. The winner was George Gilbert Scott, already the best-known Gothic Revival architect of the day. His imposing design in polychromatic brick, with a soaring spire and tower, was quite different from the first generation of railway hotels that preceded it.

The Midland Grand is undeniably extravagant inside and out. It eventually cost more than fourteen times the price of the modest Great Northern Hotel at King's Cross next door which it overlooks, but this was no doubt part of the appeal to the Midland directors. Construction started

Aerial view of St. Pancras International in 2012, showing the modern extension of the station roof (top left) and the restored hotel façade. King's Cross, with its new departures concourse roof linking the station with the Great Northern Hotel, is top right.

in 1868 when the station had already opened and the hotel was not completed until 1876. Scott had no regrets, even recording in 1870 that 'it is often spoken of to me as the finest building in London; my own belief is that it is possibly *too good* for its purpose.'

By the 1930s the hotel's high Victorian style was out of fashion and its facilities, state of the art in the 1870s, had been overtaken by the next generation of grand hotels. The LMS, which had inherited it from the Midland, turned the building into offices but made no moves to modernise the station. John Betjeman, writing in 1949 just after nationalisation, saw little hope for it: 'I have no doubt that British Railways will do away with St. Pancras altogether. It is too beautiful and romantic to survive'.

In 1967 St. Pancras was added to the national list of protected historic buildings at Grade I, but there was no sustainable conservation plan to take this forward. The answer had to wait until the early twenty-first century when two separate preservation schemes for the station and hotel came together to give new life to both.

Much of Scott's building has been converted back to its original use as a luxury hotel, now appropriately named the St. Pancras Renaissance. It occupies the main public rooms of the Midland Grand, all meticulously restored, and re-opened in 2011. The upper levels on the Euston Road frontage have been developed as luxury private apartments.

An appropriate long-term use for Barlow's trainshed has been found as the London terminus of Britain's first new main line in more than a century. When the Channel Tunnel first opened in 1994, Eurostar trains could only use the existing main line with other trains to Waterloo. In 1998, work began on HS1, a separate high-speed line from the tunnel entrance at Folkestone. It runs through Kent, then mainly in tunnel across to Essex and below east and north London, emerging close to King's Cross to curve into St. Pancras.

St. Pancras
International
five years after
opening, with
Eurostar trains,
2012.

Barlow's great trainshed has been extensively renovated, extended on track level and had its undercroft converted for passenger use. It was renamed St. Pancras International and formally re-opened by the Queen in November 2007, perhaps the grandest statement yet of a twenty-first century rail revival.

KING'S CROSS

When King's Cross opened in 1852, it was the largest railway station in Britain and much admired. Sceptical shareholders of the GNR, who muttered about extravagance in their new terminus, were told by the company chairman that it was 'the cheapest building for what it contains, and will contain, that can be pointed out in London.' He was probably right. The total construction cost of £123,500 was far less than the combined bill for the Euston Arch and Great Hall alone.

King's Cross was designed by Lewis Cubitt, younger brother of master builder Thomas Cubitt, who had developed much of London's Belgravia and Bloomsbury a few years earlier. He was apparently not related to Joseph Cubitt, chief engineer of the GNR, who worked with his namesake on the station.

King's Cross is straightforward, functional and economical, a complete contrast to the showiness of Euston just down the road and the Gothic elaboration of St. Pancras which later overshadowed it. Lewis Cubitt announced that what he wanted to achieve at King's Cross was 'fitness for purpose and the characteristic expression of that purpose'.

The GNR arrived in London in 1850, initially using a temporary station at Maiden Lane (now York Way), just north of the Regent's Canal on the site to be developed as a goods depot. While the tunnel taking the railway under the canal to the permanent passenger terminus was being built, the very basic facilities at Maiden Lane had to accommodate huge numbers of trippers visiting London from the North for the Great Exhibition of 1851. Even Queen Victoria and Prince Albert had to make do with Maiden Lane when they set off for Scotland by GNR in 1851.

The permanent King's Cross station was built on a 10-acre site formerly occupied by smallpox and fever hospitals. The Cubitts created a pair of long brick trainsheds for the arrival and departure platforms, separated by a strong arched wall.

King's Cross in 1853, soon after opening, with the Great Northern Hotel nearing completion on the left.

Going North by George Earl, 1893. Wealthy families heading for Scotland gather on the platform at King's Cross with their dogs and luggage at the start of the grouse shooting season.

Each platform hall originally had a full-length *wooden* roof, later replaced with iron and glass. At the London end are two semi-circular glazed arch windows, with a clock tower above and between them as the only decorative feature.

Just to the west, and originally quite separate from the station, is the Great Northern Hotel, a rather plain Italianate addition, also by Lewis Cubitt, that was completed in 1854. After being scheduled for demolition in the first King's Cross masterplan 150 years later, it has now been fully refurbished and physically linked to the station by the roof of the new passenger concourse completed in 2012.

The simplicity of the original station layout at King's Cross had become compromised by the rapid growth of traffic in the late nineteenth century and the lack of space to expand. As well as being the terminus for the East Coast main line to the North, King's Cross had to accommodate local passenger services from its branch lines to the north London suburbs and Hertfordshire. A sharply curved branch line down each side of the terminus took GNR suburban trains alongside the Metropolitan Railway to the City at Moorgate, but only after they had squeezed through the bottleneck of the King's Cross tunnels.

There was dark talk of the GNR's 'suburban incubus' stifling its prestigious main line services. Somehow, particularly after the LNER takeover in 1923, King's Cross maintained a more glamorous image than the LMS, particularly in their rival services to Scotland. While little was done to improve services for the LNER's long-suffering suburban commuters, the long-distance expresses were always in the news. The 'Flying Scotsman' became Britain's most famous train, non-stop to Edinburgh from 1928 and half an hour faster than the LMS trains on the hilly West Coast route from Euston to Glasgow.

The image of King's Cross as the great departure point for the North was always at odds with the reality of a rather cramped terminus with poor passenger facilities. Steam working was ended in the early 1960s, but still little was done to improve the station and its environs, which became increasingly seedy. A terrible fire on the Tube escalators in 1987 in which 31 people died seemed to confirm the area's reputation for neglect, but was also a catalyst for change.

A masterplan for the redevelopment of the whole area around King's Cross and St. Pancras was eventually prepared

King's Cross departures, with the 'Flying Scotsman' service on the right, c.1928.

King's Cross station façade, cleaned and opened up with Kings's Cross Square in front of it, 2015.

in the 1990s, but only implemented gradually in the early 2000s. A £500 million restoration plan for the main line station was announced by Network Rail in 2005 and finally completed in 2021. This involved restoring and reglazing the original arched trainsheds, removing the 1970s Travel Centre at the front of the station and clearing this area to

Platform 1 at King's Cross, with one of the station's elaborate restored clocks, 2016.

The spectacular new departures concourse at King's Cross, designed by John McAslan, 2016.

create an open-air plaza called King's Cross Square. This revealed Cubitt's elegant frontage properly for the first time in over a century. Most significantly, a spacious new semi-circular departures concourse designed by John McAslan was created on the western side of the station, covered by a spectacular single span roof engineered by Arup. This not only solves a long-standing problem of overcrowding and queues waiting for trains, but provides all passengers with an almost theatrical experience as the colours of the roof change in the darkening evening light. It has arguably turned King's Cross into London's most artistic station experience and a relaxing place to travel through or wait for a train with a coffee on the balcony.

LIVERPOOL STREET

Liverpool Street is probably the most successful large-scale heritage redevelopment in the heart of the City of London. The best aspects of an historic environment that was threatened with destruction in the 1970s have been retained and integrated with a huge modern office development that

Crowded
suburban
platforms at
Liverpool Street,
1884.

took place here in the 1980s on three sides and partly above the Victorian terminus.

Much of the station now dates from the late twentieth century but was built in late Victorian style to complement the restored and reinstated original features. Extensive demolition has also taken place, including the whole of Broad Street station next door, but this project was also a triumph of building conservation and reasonable compromise. Thirty years on it is almost impossible to distinguish genuinely old from new and reproduction, yet the result does not feel like a pastiche.

Plans for the construction of Liverpool Street were drawn up by the Great Eastern Railway (GER) soon after the company's creation in 1862. The GER was formed by merging five existing companies, which, between them, controlled all the railways in East Anglia. The largest component was the Eastern Counties Railway which had opened a London terminus at Shoreditch in 1840. This station, known as Bishopsgate from 1846, was just outside the City of London boundary and inconvenient for business travellers to London's financial centre.

Denied access to the North London Railway's (NLR) terminus at Broad Street, opened in 1865, the GER determined to build its own short extension into the City. This proved an expensive and flawed project. The NLR line ran into Broad Street at high level on a viaduct but the GER chose to build their larger Liverpool Street terminus alongside with the platforms below street level. This was to provide a rail connection with the Metropolitan Railway, a link that was in the end hardly used.

To bring the line down to this level at Liverpool Street the GER had to build the City extension up a steep bank to Bethnal Green, which created long term operating difficulties. As Lord Claud Hamilton, the GER's last chairman, acknowledged in 1923, this was a serious mistake as 'every one of our heavily laden trains has to commence its journey at the bottom of an incline.' In steam days this was quite a problem and remained so until electrification in the 1960s.

When Liverpool Street opened in 1874–5, it was laid out in an L-shape with short platforms for suburban trains on the western side and longer main-line platforms to the east. A very long and tall wrought-iron-and-glass roof consisting of two aisles and two naves gave the station a cathedral-like quality, later enhanced by an elaborate four-faced Gothic clock that hung over the tracks. The impressive roof structure was the work of Edward Wilson, the GER's engineer.

Painting by Marjorie Sherlock of Liverpool Street west side suburban platforms, c.1918, just before the Jazz Service was introduced.

LNER poster advertising the Great Eastern Hotel restaurant at Liverpool Street, c.1930, claiming it to be 'the most popular rendezvous in the City'.

THE MOST POPULAR RENDEZVOUS IN THE CITY

GREAT EASTERN HOTEL LIVERPOOL S.ᵗ STATION LONDON, E.C.2.

OWNED AND MANAGED BY THE LONDON & NORTH EASTERN RAILWAY
FOR PARTICULARS OF TARIFFS APPLY RESIDENT MANAGER

Traffic at the station grew so fast that an extension was soon required, adding eight new platforms on the east side parallel to Bishopsgate in 1894. Meanwhile the Great Eastern Hotel was completed along the Liverpool Street frontage in 1884 and also extended to double its size in 1899–1901. The Great Eastern was then the largest hotel in the City and its opulent interior included the Hamilton Hall, the Abercorn Rooms and two Masonic temples, one Grecian in style and the other Egyptian.

At the start of the twentieth century, Liverpool Street was for a time the largest and busiest London terminus. Its 18 platforms dealt with nearly 1,100 train movements every 24 hours. Although it offered long distance express services to Norwich, Cambridge and the Continent via Harwich, Liverpool Street has always primarily been a terminus for City workers. The GER deliberately built up an intensive suburban service from all over north-east London and this became its main customer base.

In 1912, when Liverpool Street got a Tube connection to the Central London Railway, the terminus above was dealing with 200,000 passengers a day. After the First World War this rose by more than 10 per cent. With no space to enlarge the station again, electrification seemed the obvious option, but the GER could not afford the high cost of modernisation. Instead the company launched an intensive new steam suburban service that doubled the number of rush-hour trains. At the height of the evening peak, 24 16-coach trains, each with 848 seats, ran in quick succession over one track on the climb from Liverpool Street to Bethnal Green. This was an amazing achievement with manual signalling and little steam tank engines. It was soon christened the 'Jazz Service' and was still known as this right up to eventual electrification in 1960.

Passenger numbers peaked in the early 1920s, allowing the GER's successor from 1923, the LNER, to postpone the inevitable electrification until after nationalisation in 1948. During its 25 years of running Liverpool Street, the LNER did virtually nothing to improve or modernise its busiest commuter station. The suburban services were not fully electrified by British Railways until 1960.

A plan to rebuild Liverpool Street completely was put forward by BR in 1975. This scheme involved closing and demolishing Broad Street next door and creating an enlarged 22-platform station across both sites, buried under a raft of commercial development. There was strong opposition to this from heritage bodies and a long public inquiry took place in 1976–7 which recommended retention of the west side trainshed and the Great Eastern Hotel. When planning permission was eventually given for redevelopment in the early 1980s, it was for a completely different scheme. Broad Street and the eastern trainshed would go but the main part of Liverpool Street and the hotel would have to be preserved and adapted rather than disappearing underground.

This was an important moment in the history of London's great termini and a novel approach to modernisation. Unlike the wholesale demolition and functional rebuild of Euston, Liverpool

Liverpool Street concourse after major reconstruction in the late 1980s. The relocated GER war memorial is top right.

Street demanded a more thoughtful and subtle approach that could blend heritage features with high-tech modernity. The new station that emerged from the six-year reconstruction in 1985–91 is a model project where co-ordination between planners, developers, architects and engineers has worked well, incorporating the best of old and new. A further improvement arrives in 2022, with the opening of the Elizabeth Line.

FENCHURCH STREET

Small – but periodically busy – Fenchurch Street was the first terminus within the square mile of the City of London. A station was opened on the present site by the London & Blackwall Railway (LBR) in 1841, just beyond the original terminus of its short 3.5-mile line. Built largely on a brick-arched viaduct, the LBR connected the Minories, on the edge of the City, with the East and West India Docks. The line was

Fenchurch Street postcard with a LT&SR train arriving, c.1912.

originally cable-hauled, powered by stationary steam engines, a system which soon proved cumbersome and unreliable. In 1849, cable traction was abandoned and the railway introduced conventional locomotive-hauled trains.

From 1850, a junction at Bow connected Fenchurch Street with the North London Railway, which began running local trains right across north London and there were soon proposals

Fenchurch Street in 1912, with a horse-drawn delivery van and early motor cars.

to bring in further traffic on new lines from Essex. This led the LBR to rebuild its terminus in partnership with the newly formed London, Tilbury & Southend Railway (LT&SR). The new station was designed by the LBR's engineer George Berkeley and opened in 1854.

Fenchurch Street station then barely changed physically for more than a century, but had a complex history of operation by several different railway companies, at various times both partners and rivals. It was the City terminus for NLR services until the company opened its own new terminus at Broad Street in 1865. In 1866, the LBR was taken over by the GER but most services at Fenchurch Street were provided by the LT&SR, itself absorbed by the MR in 1912.

Traffic at Fenchurch Street boomed in the early 1900s, with season ticket sales nearly doubling between 1902 and 1909. By the 1920s, when the LMS took over, the station was handling 50,000 passengers on weekdays, nearly all of them commuters from Metropolitan Essex. In the 1930s, passenger numbers rose again to 70,000 a day, but like the LNER, the LMS would not invest in electrification, which only finally took place in 1962.

In the 1980s, an air-space development scheme above the station gave BR sufficient income to modernise the station

Fenchurch Street station in 2021. The 1854 façade has been retained, but the inside of the station has been entirely rebuilt, with the roof removed to put new offices above.

entirely. George Berkeley's attractive 1854 façade, now listed, was preserved, but the interior was gutted and the trainshed removed to make way for an office building above. This is a stepped pyramid structure set back from the station frontage so that it does not overpower the Victorian façade visually. Escalators were installed up to an enlarged first-floor concourse with a new ticket office and retail units. The design of the station interior is bland but functional, making better use of the limited space available.

Fenchurch Street remains a curious anomaly among London's terminals. It is still the smallest of them all, with just four platforms, and the least known because of its back-street location and lack of direct Underground interchange. The station is almost exclusively used by City commuters from south Essex on weekdays and is deserted at weekends, but passenger throughput is still over 15 million a year. Post-Covid commuter patterns are certain to change as more people adapt to working partly from home, which may reduce the traditional rush hour pressures.

LONDON BRIDGE

London Bridge is on the site of the first passenger railway terminus in the capital, opened on 14 December 1836 by the Lord Mayor. The London & Greenwich Railway (L&GR) brought the first steam railway to London, but its ambitions were modest. As originally proposed the line was to be just 3.5 miles long, running between Greenwich and Tooley Street in Southwark, close to the southern end of London Bridge.

The promoters adopted a scheme designed by a retired Royal Engineer, Colonel G.T. Landmann, who suggested that the line should be built throughout on a brick-arched viaduct. Much of the route was then still in open country, mainly used for market gardening, and at high level the line could easily bridge roads at the London end and also the Surrey Canal. It was also intended that the railway arches would generate

Ticket for the opening of the capital's first passenger railway at London Bridge, December 1836.

income by being rented out as stables, workshops or even, rather optimistically, as homes.

Even before any trains started running, Landmann's 878-arch viaduct was being promoted as an entertainment to visit and stroll along the tree-lined 'boulevard' alongside. The entire length of the viaduct was illuminated by gas, making it a novel spectacle even after dark. In March 1835, *The Times* reported that more than 3,000 people had paid 1d (one old penny) each to walk on the footpath on a Sunday, which could bring in about £400 a year.

London Bridge beat Euston by seven months as the first rail entrance to London, but the station was, in Alan Jackson's words, 'a very Spartan affair'. Trains arrived and departed from two open platforms at the end of the brick viaduct. The only station building was a plain three-storey block at ground level on the south side, which contained the booking office. Up on the viaduct itself there was no trainshed, roof or weather

The exterior of London Bridge Station under Southern Railway ownership, c.1927. None of these buildings remain.

protection of any kind for waiting passengers. A design was prepared for a triumphal arch, but this was never built.

Nothing remains of the original terminus at London Bridge except for part of the viaduct structure, which can be seen at the Tooley Street end of what was formerly Joiner Street and is now a walkway under the station. London Bridge started small but grew rapidly into a large, sprawling station complex divided up between different railway companies. The little L&GR did not have aspirations itself to develop into a main line company, but saw the revenue potential in giving other railways access rights over its viaduct to London Bridge, where it owned enough land to develop a much larger terminus on its expanded site.

The machinations, mergers and fallouts between a number of competing Victorian railway companies were the cause of more than a century's chaos at London Bridge. Decisions taken in the 1850s and '60s effectively blighted its layout for 150 years. Passenger numbers more than doubled at this time from 5.5 million to more than 10 million a year as the main players effectively divided the site up between them. Two companies merged to form the London, Brighton & South

London Bridge Station in 2010, just before the 1860s station was taken down, with the Shard tower under construction behind.

Terminal platforms after complete reconstruction, 2016.

Coast Railway (LB&SCR) in 1846, which developed the southern side of the site as a terminal station. On the northern side the rival South Eastern Railway (SER) built its own station, but soon planned to extend further towards the City.

Until the recent rebuild, the most impressive thing about London Bridge was not the incoherent layout or the buildings but the railway approach. By the beginning of the twentieth century the viaduct begun in the 1830s had been widened to accommodate eleven parallel tracks. All these are still intensively used by commuter trains on a daily basis, the busiest rail approach to central London. Electric trains were first introduced here by the LB&SCR, using an overhead power supply for their South London line round to Victoria, opened in 1908. In the 1920s the Southern Railway (SR), which took over both the London Bridge rivals in 1923, began electrifying all routes into the two stations on the third rail system which has been used ever since.

The station was badly damaged by bombing in the Second World War, but only patched up afterwards. A complete reconstruction plan by BR in 1961, to be funded by commercial development above the station, was turned down. Instead there was partial and inadequate redevelopment from the late 1960s onwards, but a comprehensive modernisation plan had to wait until the twenty-first century. This was carried out by Network Rail between 2009 and 2017 and involved the rebuilding of all 15 platforms, full access by lift and escalator, the creation of two new street-level entrances and an extensive low-level concourse. Architects for the project were Grimshaw, previously responsible for the design of Waterloo International in the 1990s.

The new concourse at London Bridge, completed in 2018.

In a separate project, the impressive but controversial Shard office tower, currently the tallest structure in Europe, was completed immediately alongside the station in 2012. Rebuilding the station did require the demolition of the 1893 SER offices on the north side and the removal of the Brighton side's listed 1860s overall roof, but much of this has been carefully removed for reconstruction on the Vale of Rheidol heritage steam railway in Aberystwyth.

London Bridge has always been confusing and difficult to use, with poor access on multiple levels, but it is now a model of clarity. The signage and wayfinding on the new station is particularly clear and London Bridge no longer feels like an intimidating warren suitable only for seasoned commuters. It has also been opened up on all sides, rather than acting as a grim brick barrier dividing the local area.

CANNON STREET

Cannon Street is the product of Victorian railway rivalry. The SER, which had brought its trains from the Kent coast as far as London Bridge in 1844, was soon in competition with the London, Chatham & Dover Railway (LC&DR), which developed an alternative route to the capital across north Kent in the 1850s. When the Chatham line planned to get direct access to the City by crossing the Thames at Blackfriars, the SER secured its own route over the river to Cannon Street on a branch from its Charing Cross extension.

The station, river bridge and viaducts were all designed by John Hawkshaw, the SER's consulting engineer. Work began in July 1863 and Cannon Street was opened on 1 September 1866. Hawkshaw's station was built on a great brick-arched base structure at the northern end of the bridge over the Thames. Massive arcaded walls down both sides originally supported a crescent-shaped iron-and-glass roof over the platforms, with tall twin towers at the river end. At the other end of the trainshed was the City Terminus Hotel, built by a separate company to a design by E.M. Barry. The hotel's public rooms became popular for banquets and business gatherings including, bizarrely, the meeting in July 1920 at which the Communist Party of Great Britain was established.

Cannon Street station and rail bridge from the Thames when first completed, with St Paul's Cathedral beyond, 1866.

Cannon Street was electrified by the SR in the late 1920s and rush hour commuter traffic became its mainstay. The boat trains to Kent nearly all ran from Victoria by this time, but some steam-hauled express services left Cannon Street until the early 1960s.

The terminus and hotel were badly damaged by wartime bombs and after being patched up at the end of the war the overall roof was taken down for safety reasons in 1958. The hotel, which had become offices, was demolished in 1963. The station then went through two long phases of rebuilding in the next thirty years. Bland 1960s office blocks were built in place of the hotel and over the station concourse, which was remodelled and linked to a modernised underground station below it.

In a second phase of redevelopment, the Cannon Place development in 2010 brought better quality commercial offices over the station frontage. The main-line station platforms were left open to the sky until the late 1980s, when a separate office development on a steel deck was inserted between the remains of the great walls. The smoke-blackened Victorian brickwork and the twin towers were cleaned and now bookend the black-and-white prow of the new commercial offices on top of the station.

Cannon Street with the City towers beyond, 2020.

BLACKFRIARS

The next rail crossing of the Thames is at Blackfriars, just upriver beyond Southwark Bridge. The first railway bridge here was built by the SER's great rival, the LC&DR, in 1864. This original bridge was dismantled in 1985, leaving only the iron support piers and granite plinths. The LC&DR opened a station called Blackfriars on the south bank, and started running its first trains over the river to Ludgate Hill in 1865. A few months later, the line was extended to join up with the Metropolitan Railway at Farringdon. This was the first and only railway permitted to cross central London in the nineteenth century, but was soon used mainly for goods traffic rather than passenger trains. The LC&DR built a spur to a new terminus at Holborn Viaduct in 1874 and built a second railway bridge over the river in the 1880s to another new terminus on the north bank called St. Paul's. The company had unrealistic aspirations and had the stonework on the frontage inscribed with 54 domestic and foreign destinations, including Bromley and Broadstairs, but also Baden Baden and Brindisi, the mundane to the romantic.

The LC&DR was unable to survive as an independent company and in 1899 was forced to merge with its more

The original Blackfriars Station on the south bank of the Thames in 1863, before construction of a new terminus on the north bank when a second railway bridge was opened in the 1880s.

powerful long-term competitor, the SER, to form the South Eastern & Chatham Railway (SECR). This in turn became part of the SR in 1923 and St. Paul's station, renamed Blackfriars in 1937, abandoned its overseas destinations and settled down to being a minor part of the Southern Electric network.

Having survived the Blitz, though with considerable bomb damage, Blackfriars continued as a small commuter terminus until the Thameslink programme, first developed by BR in the 1980s, revived the idea of a north-south passenger railway through London. Holborn Viaduct was closed as a terminus in 1990, replaced by a new through station at nearby Ludgate Hill called City Thameslink when cross-London services were first revived.

Blackfriars was to become pivotal in the development of the long-delayed Thameslink programme. The station was extensively rebuilt between 2009 and 2012 in a project that involved building new through platforms extending right across the river bridge which could accommodate 12-car trains and a second station entrance on the south side of the river close to the popular Tate Modern gallery, which had opened in 2000. The station now has a stylish entrance hall at the City end, glazing right across both sides of the bridge and 4,400 photovoltaic panels on the long platform roof over the river. Blackfriars has belatedly taken on a key position in the establishment of Thameslink as a

Blackfriars Station on the north bank, c.1993, before the station was rebuilt and extended out across the bridge itself.

London, Chatham & Dover Railway iron decoration from the first bridge at Blackfriars, with the new station, the Tate Modern and the Shard behind.

Blackfriars station from Tate Modern after extension right across the railway bridge to a second entrance on the South Bank, 2017. The platforms are now glazed and the entire roof covered with photo-voltaic panels.

north-south cross-London project which opens up London's railway network in a way that will soon be complemented by the Elizabeth Line from east to west.

CHARING CROSS

Charing Cross is the only main-line terminus conveniently serving the West End of London, being just a few minutes walk from Whitehall, Piccadilly and Covent Garden. It was a late arrival, opening in 1864 as a result of the SER's determination to compete with the rival LC&DR, which ran to Victoria, in offering a well-placed new station for its continental boat trains to the Kent coast. They built an extension from their London Bridge station that ran west across Southwark at high level. A new City branch off this extension to Cannon Street and a link with the London & South Western Railway (LSWR) terminus at Waterloo were all part of the SER's ambitious growth plan.

For its terminus site, the SER acquired Hungerford Market, at the western end of the Strand, and for its river crossing took over and dismantled the Charing Cross Suspension Bridge, built by I.K. Brunel in 1845. To carry trains over the Thames the SER's engineer, Sir John Hawkshaw, designed the exceptionally ugly but extremely solid Hungerford Bridge, which incorporated a replacement footbridge to Brunel's on its downstream side. One of the most successful of the Millennium projects in London was the addition of elegant new matching independent suspension footbridges on both sides of the rail bridge, dramatically improving the riverscape at this point by effectively hiding the rail bridge. These were opened in 2003.

Hawkshaw was also responsible for the design of Charing Cross station, which originally had a long, tall arched trainshed over the platforms. At the river end the approach over the bridge is elevated, with the Strand end of the station at ground level because of the steep rise from the river shore. The Embankment was built along the Thames in the 1860s, incorporating both main drainage for London and the District

Charing Cross station interior, South Eastern Railway, opened in 1864.

Barry's Charing Cross Hotel from the Strand, with his reimagined Eleanor Cross in the forecourt, all completed for the SER in 1864. This modern view shows the bland postwar upper floors of the hotel, which replaced the bomb-damaged Victorian roof.

Railway, which opened a separate station here in 1870.

Across the Strand frontage, E.M. Barry designed the imposing French Renaissance-style Charing Cross Hotel, opened in 1865. Many of the sumptuous Victorian public rooms are happily still intact, though the top floors of the hotel were replaced after wartime bombing with a drab neo-Georgian addition that is quite unsympathetic to Barry's elaborate façade. In the station forecourt is an imaginative reconstruction, also by Barry, of the memorial to Queen Eleanor that was erected in Whitehall soon after her death in 1290, but destroyed by Puritans in 1647. The story of the building of the medieval Charing Cross is told pictorially in a remarkable set of mural panels designed by David Gentleman in 1979 that run the full length of the Northern Line Tube platforms below.

In 1899, the SER and its great rival, the LC&DR, combined to form the South Eastern & Chatham Railway and began operating Charing Cross as a joint concern. In December 1905, the main part of the station roof collapsed suddenly during maintenance work, killing six people. The cause was found to be a structural weakness in one of the wrought-iron tie rods, which had fractured. The SECR decided to replace Hawkshaw's roof completely with a flat steel girder design.

During the First World War, the SECR played an important strategic role as the British railway running closest to the Western Front. Many troop trains left Charing Cross for Dover and Folkestone, and ambulance trains returned here with growing numbers of casualties. Charing Cross became more important as a commuter station between the wars, when the SR electrified the suburban network inherited from the SECR in 1923.

Dramatic change came under British Rail management in the 1980s, when a huge air-space development project called Embankment Place was created both over and under the station. The office development is not visible from the Strand

elevation but from the Embankment the bulky post-modern office structure, designed by Terry Farrell & Partners, is now the dominant building along this part of the river.

Charing Cross from the platforms, 1904. This is the original overall roof that collapsed in 1905.

Inside the station the passenger concourse is still naturally toplit through a glazed roof and has been fully refurbished, with the retention of the double-faced Victorian station clock. Beyond the barriers the platforms are now almost entirely rafted over, with an oppressively low ceiling cutting out all natural light. Charing Cross now looks its best from a distance, particularly when viewed over the river at night from the South Bank.

Charing Cross from the bridge in 2010, showing the post-modern office development Embankment Place built over the station in the 1980s.

WATERLOO

Waterloo was the butt of music hall jokes in the nineteenth century, with a reputation as London's most confusing railway station. Its appearance in *Three Men In A Boat*, published in 1896, is a typical comic characterisation. Heading for Kingston-upon-Thames for a leisurely river trip, the heroes arrive at Waterloo by cab and ask where the eleven-five starts from. 'Of course nobody knew; nobody ever does know where a train is going to start from, or where a train when it does start is going to, or anything about it.' Eventually, they bribe an engine driver to make sure his train goes to Kingston. 'We learned afterwards that the train we had come by was really the Exeter mail, and that they had spent hours at Waterloo looking for it.'

This was an exaggeration of course, but the operation of Waterloo had become sufficiently chaotic for the LSWR to decide that complete reconstruction of their sprawling station was the only way forward. This took more than 20 years to achieve, but it created Britain's first and best-laid out twentieth-century terminus, the only one that could take both holiday traffic and a huge daily tide of commuters in its stride.

Waterloo was not the original terminus of the first main line from the south west. The London & Southampton Railway, promoted in 1831, opened its route as far as Woking in 1838, reaching Southampton in 1840. The London terminus was at Nine Elms, just south of Vauxhall Bridge and close to a river pier that was convenient for goods transfer on to barges. It also gave passengers onward access to the City by steamboat, and there were horse bus connections with other parts of central London. But the railway company, renamed the LSWR in 1839, soon recognised the benefits of extending closer to central London.

The extension of just under two miles to the south end of Waterloo Bridge was built mainly on a brick viaduct. Waterloo station was built well above street level at the end of the viaduct, with provision for further extension towards the City. No proper station buildings were erected in the early years but the terminus grew with extra platforms added in an almost haphazard fashion. On the west side, what became known as the Windsor station, dealing with the Windsor lines and other local traffic, first opened in 1860.

On the eastern side of the approach, a separate private station was opened in 1854 by the London Necropolis Company, which ran a daily funeral train right into its cemetery beside the main line at Brookwood, near Woking. Brookwood quickly became the largest cemetery in the world, but the one-way traffic from Waterloo did not become the main solution to Victorian London's growing burial problems, as its promoters had hoped. The Necropolis terminus was reconstructed in 1902 with a new entrance building on Westminster Bridge Road. This still survives as offices, but the Necropolis station and funeral train service were closed down after taking a direct hit in an air raid in 1941.

'The Gateway to Health & Pleasure', an LSWR poster featuring the newly completed Victory Arch at Waterloo, opened by Queen Mary in 1922.

The radical reconstruction of Waterloo was planned by the LSWR's new chief engineer, J.W. Jacomb Hood, who was appointed in 1901. He designed the new station after a study visit to look at the latest railway terminals being built in the United States. Jacomb Hood proposed a large station with 23 platforms and a wide passenger concourse, all on a new superstructure, with a steel-framed frontage block housing the main facilities such as the booking hall, cloakrooms and tea rooms.

Jacomb Hood died in 1914 before the station rebuild was finished, and his successor, A.W. Szlumper, finished the job. Electrification of the LSWR's suburban lines on the third rail system began just before the First World War, with the first electric trains running from Waterloo to Wimbledon via East Putney in 1915. Completion of the station rebuilding and further electrification was inevitably delayed by the war, but the opening of the Victory Arch by Queen Mary in 1922 was a triumphant occasion for the LSWR as it prepared for takeover by the SR at the 1923 Grouping.

The SR had less reliance on freight traffic than the other three main-line companies and developing better commuter services to London was the obvious way to go. By the 1930s all suburban services into Waterloo and the main line to Portsmouth had been electrified. Waterloo had become London's busiest and most up-to-date station.

When a day in the life of Waterloo was observed by film director John Schlesinger in his classic 1961 documentary *Terminus*, he captured many everyday scenes that were to disappear by the end of the 1960s: an army of porters meeting the boat trains from Southampton; the departure of the all-Pullman *Bournemouth Belle*; the arrival of Afro-Caribbean migrants in London; and main-line steam locomotives running alongside the ubiquitous suburban electrics. With appropriate

Waterloo by Helen McKie, celebrating the station's centenary in 1948, and depicting the station during the Second World War. This was the last poster produced by the Southern Railway before nationalisation.

timing, the final steam-hauled services departed in July 1967, just as the Kinks' London lament 'Waterloo Sunset' reached the top of the pop charts.

In the 1990s, a new terminus for Eurostar services from the Channel Tunnel was built on the north-western side of Waterloo, replacing the Windsor line platforms. The Eurostar trains are twice the length of most standard British express trains and required double-length platforms. Nicholas Grimshaw & Partners came up with a spectacular design that is a modern interpretation of the traditional Victorian trainshed, snaking down the side of Waterloo's rectangular Edwardian roof and extending in a gentle curve beyond it.

Eurostar train in the new Waterloo International terminal opened in 1994. This became redundant when HS1 opened to St. Pancras in 2007, but was eventually adapted and reopened for domestic services in 2019.

This brilliant piece of architectural engineering was delivered on schedule in 1993, but not opened until 1994, when the delayed Channel Tunnel project was completed. Waterloo International then had a working life of just 13 years. The Eurostar trains needed a dedicated high-speed line, but were having to share existing tracks to Waterloo. When Britain's first high-speed line (HS1) was built across Kent from 1998, a different route under the Thames and across east and north London to St. Pancras was chosen. When HS1 opened in November 2007, Waterloo International became redundant and lay unused for 12 years before reopening for domestic services – an expensive tribute to poor government planning and decision making.

VICTORIA

Victoria was built originally as two separate stations alongside each other by two companies, later combined uncomfortably into one. John Betjeman memorably called it 'London's most conspicuous monument to commercial rivalry'.

Arrival of a
workmen's train
at Victoria, 1865.

The Victoria
frontage in 1910,
showing the
separately rebuilt
Edwardian
façades of the
SECR (left) and
the LB&SCR
(centre) with the
Grosvenor Hotel
at the end of the
station façade.

None of the early terminals for main lines from the south was conveniently located for the City or Westminster. London Bridge, Bricklayers Arms and Waterloo were all south of the river, and the rival companies jostling for access to central London looked for an alternative way in to the west. A proposal by a new company, the Victoria Station & Pimlico Railway, to build a short connecting line over the river at Battersea to a new terminal site in Pimlico was approved in 1858. Two of the main southern companies, the LB&SCR and the LC&DR agreed to use the VS&PR tracks over the new Grosvenor Bridge and took long leases on two sides of the station site in Pimlico, which was named Victoria.

Twin terminals were built with a dividing wall between, the LB&SCR station opening in 1860 and the LC&DR two years later. They were run quite independently and there was no physical connection between them, to the confusion of many travellers. Victoria's split personality is acknowledged in the well known 'handbag' episode in Oscar Wilde's *The Importance of Being Earnest*, first performed in 1895. Jack tries to bolster his account of being found as a baby in the cloakroom at Victoria station with the added detail of its specific location on the Brighton side. This elicits Lady Bracknell's dismissive response: 'The *line* is immaterial'.

Neither the Brighton nor the Chatham company bothered to add any architectural embellishment to the frontage of their respective trainsheds at Victoria. Wooden buildings and boarding gave both station entrances a shabby, temporary appearance that remained unchanged for more than forty years. An imposing Renaissance style grand hotel, the Grosvenor, was opened alongside the Brighton station in 1861, but ran independently of the railway. This gave Victoria its only real architectural presence in the nineteenth century.

The LB&SCR eventually modernised its frontage in the early 1900s, buying the Grosvenor in 1899 and extending the hotel at right angles across the station frontage. The rather pompous new Edwardian baroque wing of the hotel opened in 1907 and included much-improved passenger facilities on the concourse inside the station, all designed by the LB&SCR's engineer, Charles Morgan. Many of the decorative details survive, including two previously hidden tile maps of the railway's main line and suburban systems in one of the entrance passageways.

At the other end, the Brighton platforms were extended towards the river, allowing each of them to accommodate two trains at once, effectively doubling capacity.

Changing the name of the 'Southern Belle' to the 'Brighton Belle' at Victoria when new electric Pullman trains were introduced, 1934.

BR Southern poster advertising the *Golden Arrow* Pullman service from London Victoria to Paris, 1959.

Improved train services followed two years later, when the first stage of suburban electrification was introduced by the LB&SCR using the overhead wire system on its south London line round to London Bridge.

Not to be outdone, the SECR built an even more ostentatious frontage to its station next door. The building, designed by architect Arthur Blomfield, was lower than the LB&SCR's hotel extension but was deliberately set forward from its neighbour and was faced entirely in white Portland stone. Appropriately, as the entrance to the SECR's main boat train terminus, the wide central archway was set in a French Second Empire style surround, with maritime decoration including four statuesque mermaid caryatids. Inside, the old Chatham trainshed over the platforms was left untouched.

The SR took over both Victoria terminals in 1923 and started what was to be a long process of integration by knocking holes through the dividing wall. The LB&SCR's 'Elevated Electric' system was quickly abandoned and both stations were electrified on the LSWR's third-rail system, now branded as 'Southern Electric'. The rapid extension of the suburban electric network nearly doubled commuter traffic into Victoria, with middle-class season ticket holders making a daily journey from Surrey, Kent or Sussex.

The SR found a growing market for its boat train services from Victoria, not yet electrified but given the glamour and luxury of Pullman coaches and sleeping cars. The all-Pullman *Golden Arrow* was introduced in 1929, linking with a Channel crossing from Dover to Calais, where its French equivalent, the *Fleche d'Or*, took passengers on to Paris. In 1936 the *Night Ferry* was inaugurated – a luxury train of *Wagons-Lits* sleeping cars that was loaded onto a special train ferry across the Channel to Dunkirk and then ran straight through to Paris Gare du Nord.

Imperial Airways opened its art-deco London headquarters and terminal building alongside Victoria on Buckingham Palace Road. On 6 June 1939, the first SR Flying Boat train left for Southampton, but with the outbreak of war in September most civil aviation was suspended. Rail-air services only began to develop with the opening of a new station at Gatwick Airport in 1958 and London's first rail-air terminal at Victoria in 1962. The non-stop Gatwick Express was introduced in 1984.

The rise of rail-air services was matched by declining patronage of Victoria's boat trains in the 1970s. The last *Golden Arrow* ran in 1972 and the *Night Ferry* was withdrawn in 1980. As its international atmosphere faded, the station became ever busier with commuters. It needed comprehensive reorganisation to a single, logical plan but commercial pressures and opportunities led British Rail to base the selective redevelopment of Victoria

The listed 1860s roof of the Chatham side at Victoria, designed by John Fowler, then also engineer to the Metropolitan Railway.

in the early 1980s largely around exploitation of the air space over half the station. Most of the Brighton side was covered with a steel-and-concrete raft, on which first an undistinguished office block and then a glitzy shopping mall were built.

The main concourse and eastern side of the station, where the listed LC&DR roof remains, have been spruced up but not properly integrated. As London's second-busiest main-line terminal, Victoria now feels tired and neglected, particularly when compared with the more recent comprehensive refurbishment of King's Cross and London Bridge.

RAILWAY COMPANIES

GCR: Great Central Railway
GER: Great Eastern Railway
GNR: Great Northern Railway
GWR: Great Western Railway
L&BR: London & Birmingham Railway
LBR: London & Blackwall Railway (LBR to differentiate from L&BR above)
L&GR: London & Greenwich Railway
LB&SCR: London, Brighton & South Coast Railway
LC&DR: London, Chatham and Dover Railway
LMS: London, Midland & Scottish Railway
LNER: London & North Eastern Railway
LNWR: London & North Western Railway
LSWR: London & South Western Railway
LT&SR: London, Tilbury & Southend Railway
MR: Midland Railway
MS&LR: Manchester, Sheffield & Lincolnshire Railway
NLR: North London Railway
SECR: South Eastern & Chatham Railway
SER: South Eastern Railway
SR: Southern Railway

FURTHER READING

Betjeman, John. *London's Historic Railway Stations.*
  Capital Transport, 2002.
Biddle, Gordon. *Britain's Historic Railway
  Buildings.* OUP, 2003.
Bradley, Simon. *St. Pancras Station.* Profile Books, 2007.
Brindle, Steven. *Paddington Station, its History and
  Architecture.* English Heritage, 2013.
Course, Edwin. *London Railways.* Batsford, 1962.
Darley, Peter. *The King's Cross Story.* The
  History Press, 2018.
Green, Oliver. *London's Great Railway Stations.*
  Frances Lincoln, 2021.
Jackson, Alan. *London's Termini.* David & Charles, 1969.
Jenkins, Simon. *Britain's 100 Best Railway
  Stations.* Viking 2017.
Lansley, Alastair. *The Transformation of St Pancras Station.*
  Laurence King, 2008.
Simmons, Jack. *St Pancras Station.* Historical
  Publications, 2003.
Thorne, Robert. *Liverpool Street Station.* Academy
  Editions, 1978.
White. H.P. *A Regional History of the Railways of Great
  Britain: Vol 3 Greater London.* David & Charles, 1971.
Wolmar, Christian. *Cathedrals of Steam.*
  Atlantic Books, 2020.

INDEX

LONDON'S RAILWAY STATIONS

London's railway termini are among the most recognisable and familiar landmarks in the city. Famed for their bustling platforms and architectural innovation, they comprise a fascinating mixture of Neo-Gothic exuberance and purposeful modernity. Though each owes its existence to a long-extinct Victorian railway company, these stations continue to be central to London life, with millions of visitors passing through every year. This historical whistlestop tour takes you on a circuit of London's thirteen great railway termini, from Paddington, through King's Cross, to Victoria. Ranging from the earliest stations to the latest restorations and ongoing developments, this beautifully illustrated book examines both their legacy and their future.

Oliver Green is former Head Curator of the London Transport Museum and is now its Research Fellow. He has lectured and published extensively on transport art, design and history. His books for Shire include *The Tube: Station to Station on the London Underground* and *Trams and Trolleybuses*.

www.shirebooks.co.uk

SHIRE PUBLICATIONS

ISBN 978-1-78442-505-0

5 1 4 0 0

9 781784 425050

www.shirebooks.co.uk

UK £8.99 | US $14.00 | CAN $19.00